MOVING THE CHURCH IN 7 STEPs

IMPLEMENTATION GUIDE

DAVID B. NEWELL

Copyright © 2017 – David B. Newell

All rights reserved. No part of this book may be used or reproduced in any manner, stored in a retrieval system, or transmitted in any form or by any means—electronic, mechanical, photocopy, recording, scanning or any other—except in the case of brief quotations in printed reviews, without the prior written permission from the author. Scripture quotations are taken from THE HOLY BIBLE, NEW INTERNATIONAL VERSION®, NIV® Copyright © 1973, 1978, 1984, 2011 by Biblica, Inc.™ Used by permission. All rights reserved worldwide. Emphasis within Scripture is the author's own.

Scotland Media Group
3583 Scotland Road, Building 70
Scotland PA 17254

Book ISBN: 978-1-941746-40-0
eBook ISBN: 978-1-941746-41-7

For Worldwide Distribution
Printed in the United States

1 2 3 4 5 6 7 / 21 20 19 18 17

CONTENTS

Seminar I 1

Seminar II 17

Seminar III: 27

SEMINAR IV 37

SEMINAR V 43

SEMINAR VI 49

SEMINAR VII 51

S.T.E.P. 1
STRATEGIC FOUNDATION
Seminar I

Scripture: Matthew 28:19-20, Acts 1:8, 1Corinthians 9:22

Focus: To discover potential evangelistic audiences of strategic importance.

Aim:
1. To introduce the class to the problems we face in evangelistic effectiveness.
2. To prayerfully identify potential evangelistic targets
3. Determine Spiritual Giftedness and Catalogue ALL participants

Welcome and prayer:

PRAY FOR THE GUIDANCE OF THE HOLY SPIRIT

Introduction: A few words and definitions:

Strategy: A careful plan or method for achieving a goal, usually over a long period of time.

Church: The collection of souls of those professing Jesus Christ as Savior in all its diversity of doctrines, denominations, languages, and personalities.

Audience: The specific people or persons, groups of people, or segments of society who are identified for evangelistic outreach.

What to Expect in the Course:

The course will challenge the way some think and plan evangelistic strategies. The participant should expect a great deal of interaction with other participants in formulating the best possible opportunities for outreach. Potential "audiences" will be arrived at through a collaborative approach. Inherent in such an approach is a little give and take on the part of each participant. Not every participant will be happy with the strategies chosen, but needs to give the best effort in carrying out the objectives chosen. The earlier sessions may take up to three hours to complete, but are foundational to the entire system. It is advisable to not rush the process. Find a pleasant and comfortable location to hold the seminars and provide beverages and some snacks if practical.

- This session is designed to introduce the class to the need for effective evangelistic strategies.
- That followers are instructed to evangelize is plainly seen in Scripture.
- How that mission is accomplished however depends upon the specific targets a church seeks to engage.
- While many techniques exist, too many churches are only marginally effective in significantly impacting their communities evangelistically.
- This course sets out to change that.

One session for each STEP may not be enough. It is better to be thorough over forced within specific time parameters. Some participants will not be happy with a section that drags on. However, it is important to stress the need to be fluid to enjoy success.

THINK-PAIR-SHARE

Have participants pair up and discuss the questions below. There are no wrong answers. Each group will pick a spokesperson for their group and share observations with the entire class.

Discussion Questions:

1. What do you think of when you hear "Evangelism?"
2. What has been your ministry experience with evangelism in the past?
3. What are some of the evangelistic experiences you have been involved in?
4. What has the impact of evangelism been upon your life?
5. What excites you about evangelism?
6. What scares you?

_____
_____
_____
_____
_____
_____
_____

I. Evangelistic Strategies of the Past:

Revivals, Evangelism Explosion, Concerts, Friendship Evangelism, Event and attractional approaches, are typical outreach strategies. The S.T.E.P.s will take you to the next level.

The goal of the project is to develop and implement a strategic and integrative approach to evangelism that is effective in reaching a variety of subcultures.

Our country is no longer a monolithic collection of homogeneous citizens. It is instead, a hugely diversified populace with a wide variety of ethnic groups, interests, likes, dislikes, behavioral patterns, purchasing preferences, and religious interests, etc.

Our culture is a collection of growing subcultures, each with characteristics and traits unique to them.

Watch: *Booktalk* Video

Each subculture represents an area of interest and affinity. There is often a language, attitude, and nomenclature, associated with each subculture.

People invest thousands of dollars in subculture related events, clothing, books, magazines and the like. Those points of interest represent an opportunity to the church that they may not have seized upon strategically.

SHERLOCK the ROOM:

Look around at the participants. Observe clothing, hair, hair style, hands, hats, purses, phones, phone covers, posture, markings, labels, shoes, or anything else about them from which deductions may be made, about their lives and points of interest. Ask for volunteers, to share their observations and deductions.

II. Existing Roadblocks

Many of our churches are largely ineffective at penetrating those subcultures with the Gospel. There is no "one size fits all" evangelistic approach that is effective in every subculture every time. Yet, many churches tend to continue to use models of evangelism from bygone eras and then wonder why we see little impact in society at large. Some suggest that the traditional church is no longer the vessel for effective outreach. Antiquated ideas, lack of understanding about shifts and trends in culture and associated behavioral patterns, power struggles, preconceived notions about the culture, internal struggles, fear of change, lack of innovation, short term event driven efforts, and a failure to strategically plan, all contribute to marginal evangelistic effectiveness in many churches today.

J. Stewart Black and Hal B. Gregersen suggest that most people and organizations function according to their mental maps. Those maps keep them from obtaining an accurate view of reality. They ask three questions that churches should ask as well:

1. Why, when opportunities or threats stare people in the face, do people fail to see the need to change?
2. Even when people do see the need, why do they often still fail to move?
3. Even when people move, why do they fail to finish-not going far or fast enough?

Black, Stewart J. and Gregersen, Hal B. Leading Strategic Change. (New Jersey: Prentice Hall, 2003) 8.

Many within the Church are not effective at understanding social trends and capitalizing on them. Business and industry on the other hand, invest significant resources into understanding specific markets to maximize their market share in target demographics. Because their economic survival depends upon information about their market, many have become very effective at communicating to the subcultures to whom they wish to bring their products and services, and make strategic adjustments to hold or expand their markets.

The church is only marginally aware of the vast nuances in the wide array of consumer markets. But it does not have to stay that way. The local church can once again be effective in its own back yard. To accomplish that end, a local body will need to strategically gather information about their target audience, and determine the best approach for that specific audience. Holding a tent revival for a group of bikers will most likely be ineffective. Going door to door with the "Four Spiritual Laws" in some neighborhoods may prove more harmful than good. A city wide evangelistic crusade may attract more churched than unchurched people. Efforts to develop relationships with people with whom you share no common ground, may only lead to greater frustration, resentment towards Christians and a sense of failure and guilt for the faithful member.

The approaches mentioned above are not in themselves wrong of course. They may have worked at times in a particular way. They may yet be effective in some context.

The question is not so much the methodology but choosing the best methodology for the right situation at the proper time and right place. To establish which approach is most effective, at the right time, in the right way, with optimal opportunity for success, requires significant work. There is also some trial and error in the process. Nurturing the atmosphere where failure is viewed as a stepping stone to success, requires a frame that encourages risk.

It seems as if many churches are not willing to do the hard, strategic work needed to gain all the information necessary to target specific segments and thereby ensure evangelistic effectiveness. Far too often, simply choosing a tried method of a by gone era is the option of choice. Others may attempt to look like some other church without the DNA to execute.

NOTES/THOUGHTS/INSIGHTS/PRAYERS:

Seminar I Cont.

III. Our Objective

The S.T.E.P.s is interested in developing an integrative approach to evangelism that can readily be adapted strategically to fit virtually any given need. The methodology is based upon the assumption that an integrative approach, built upon accurate research and effective implementation, would most likely increase the quantity of people brought to Jesus Christ through the ministry of the local church.

The Problem of Today:

Leslie Newbigin writes that **"if the gospel is to be understood, if it is to be received as something that communicates truth about the real human condition, if it is, as we say, to "make sense," it has to be communicated in the language of those to whom it is addressed and has to be clothed in symbols which are meaningful to them."** Leslie Newbigin, The Gospel and Pluralistic Society. (Grand Rapids: Eerdmans, 1989), 141.

Some newer models of evangelism focus upon meeting needs as the door to connecting. For the most part, American culture is affluent and needs may not be the best focal point for connecting. Common interests may make more sense as a connecting point with people.

The American culture is increasingly segmented into groups based on ethnicity, common bonds, social position, interest, cultural and social considerations, and a whole host of additional criteria. The ability of the local church to effectively communicate the gospel will be proportional to its ability to speak the "language" of those diverse groups. A "one size fits all" approach to evangelism will not yield the desired results.

BRAINSTORMING

LEVERAGING YOUR EXISTING CONTACTS

Contacts are those individuals from your circle of influence. They could be co-workers, family members, friends, social club, hobby enthusiasts, or anyone with whom participants have had some degree of connection. It is important that all participants in the Seven Steps Seminar, complete the questionnaire as thoroughly as possible. It is possible that patterns will begin to develop that show previously unknown connections. The higher the connection rate, or "saturation", the greater the likelihood of influence.

This is a process where you brainstorm and consider all the contact possibilities.

STEP 1

A. Think of any list you have in your possession. It could be email lists of people, Facebook friends, Instagram, twitter, blog followers, social groups, work relationships, neighbors, etc. This list could be considered a "warm" list.

B. Create a second list from your immediate community. This list could be considered your "cold" list. (Chamber of Commerce members, vendors, business owners, school officials etc.)

C. Pool those lists. Write the list down on a white board. Look for connections. The list may be very extensive. The greater the number, the better. Think of the process of building a funnel. Gather as many as you can and make special note of repeats.

STEP 2

A. Are there participants who possess or provide knowledge, skill, or service for whom others routinely seek?

B. Are there participants who are sought out for their advice?

C. Are there "warm" civic leaders?

STEP 3

A. Share points of contact, stories, insights participants may have about any of the names provided. Take your time and allow more than one session to complete this exorcise. The more time invested here, the greater the likelihood at forming a solid list of potential audiences.

B. Consider if a pattern has begun to emerge.

C. List the most likely from the list, with whom a relationship could be most easily formed.

Note: The purpose of the exercise is to get a large group of contacts that can be placed in a relationship funnel. It may also point to strategic associations or activities in which participants may wish to engage. Allow open conversation about the process just completed. Encourage having people share their thoughts and insights.

IV. Follow-Up for Consideration

1. What hobbies, interests, organizations, or groups do you have an interest in?

2. How do you invest your time and resources into the hobby, interest, or group?

3. What potential points of contact are within your area of interest?

4. Of those groups, what percentage of non-Christian, unchurched, or de-churched people with whom you associate?

5. How could your interests, hobbies, organizations, or groups, serve as evangelistic entry points?

6. What potential problems do you see?

7. How can potential problems be overcome?

Personal Evangelistic Style

1. Record your response to each of the 36 statements according to whether you think the statement applies to you:

    3   Very much

    2   Somewhat

    1   Very little

    0   Not at all

Transfer your responses to the grid at the bottom of the page and total each column:

____ 1. In conversations, I like to approach topics directly, without much small talk or beating around the bush.

____ 2. I have a hard time getting out of bookstores or libraries without getting a bunch of books that will help me better understand issues being debated in society.

____ 3. I often tell stories about my personal experiences in order to illustrate a point I am trying to make.

____ 4. I am a people person who places a high value on friendship.

____ 5. I enjoy including or adding new people to activities I am involved in.

____ 6. I see needs in people's lives that others often overlook.

____ 7. I do not shy away from putting people on the spot when it seems necessary.

____ 8. I tend to be analytical.

____ 9. I often identify with others by using phrases like "I used to think that too" or "I once felt the same way you do."

____ 10. other people have commented about my ability for developing new friendships.

____ 11. To be honest, even if I know the answers, I am more comfortable having someone "better qualified" explain Christianity to my friends.

____ 12. I find fulfillment in helping others, often in behind the scene ways.

____ 13. I do not have a problem confronting my friends with the truth even if it risks hurting the relationship.

____ 14. In conversation, I naturally focus on the questions that are holding up a person's spiritual progress.

____ 15. When I tell people of how I came to Christ, I have found that they have been interested in hearing it.

____ 16. I would rather delve into the personal life issues than abstract theological ideas.

____ 17. If I knew of a high-quality outreach event that my friends would enjoy, I would make a big effort to bring them.

____ 18. I prefer to show love through my actions more than my words.

____ 19. I prefer to show that real love often means telling someone the truth, even when it hurts.

____ 20. I enjoy discussions and debates on difficult questions.

____ 21. I intentionally share my mistakes with others when it will help them relate to the solutions I have found.

____ 22. I prefer getting involved in discussions concerning a person's life before dealing with the details of their beliefs.

____ 23. I tend to watch for spiritually strategic events to bring people to.

_____ 24. When people are spiritually closed, I have found that my quiet demonstrations of Christian love sometimes makes them more receptive.

_____ 25. A motto that would fit me is: "Make a difference or a mess, but do something."

_____ 26. I often get frustrated with people when they use weak arguments or poor logic.

_____ 27. People seem interested in hearing stories about things that have happened in my life.

_____ 28. I enjoy talks with friends.

_____ 29. I am always looking for a match between the needs and interests of my friends and the various events, books, etc., that they would enjoy or benefit from.

_____ 30. I feel more comfortable physically assisting a person in the name of Christ than getting involved in religious discussions.

_____ 31. I sometimes get into trouble for lacking gentleness and sensitivity in the way I interact with others.

_____ 32. I like to get at the underlying reasons for opinions that people hold.

_____ 33. I am still amazed at how God brought me to faith in him and I am motivated to tell people about it.

_____ 34. People generally consider me to be an interactive, sensitive, and caring kind of person.

_____ 35. A highlight of my week would be to take a guest with me to an appropriate church event.

_____ 36. I tend to be more practical and action oriented than philosophical and idea oriented.

Confronta-tion	Intellectual	Testimonial	Interper-sonal	Invitational	Serving
#1	#2	#3	#4	#5	#6
#7	#8	#9	#10	#11	#12
#13	#14	#15	#16	#17	#18
#19	#20	#21	#22	#23	#24
#25	#26	#27	#28	#29	#30
#31	#32	#33	#34	#35	#36
Totals					

(Mittleberg, Mark, Lee Strobel, and Bill Hybels, Becoming a Contagious Christian. Grand Rapids, MI. Zondervan, 1995. 15-18)

S.T.E.P. 2
TARGETED AUDIENCE
Seminar II

Scripture: 1 Corinthians. 9:22

Focus: To gather initial intelligence about potential audiences.

Aim:
1. The participants will continue to "brain storm" for potential evangelistic opportunities.
2. Gather information on possible audiences.
3. Determine strategies for gathering additional critical intelligence about potential audiences.

Introduction:

The examples given in the primer section may be successful methods, but certainly do not reflect the level of strategic application that is possible. Keep in mind that some strategies may be covert in nature. Depending upon the audience, there may be a strategic initiative in which the strategy does not have full participation within the church, or even function with their knowledge. For example, leveraging a connecting point with a Muslim may require longer strategy of building trust with one individual, before bringing an evangelistic introduction of Christ to them.

Welcome and prayer

To spark the engine of creativity and innovation, a list of what other churches have or are doing will be offered. In Building a Contagious Church, Mark Mittleberg catalogues the approaches of a number of different churches for each of the evangelistic categories they use.

Primer

The Confrontational style:

One church offers a "Mugging Ministry" where visitors receive a coffee mug filled with items that have the churches name on them. Another church did a "Direct Touch Ministry" where they surveyed area homes to ascertain the level of involvement in a church.

A "Back to Basics" ministry of where each month people are invited to a meal and hear a gospel presentation and receive information about the church. Men's Retreats are used by another church to aggressively share their faith with high powered speakers in a retreat setting.

A "Thing-a-ma-jig" is held by another church, which is really a youth overnight lock in which the gospel is presented at some point in the evening. Another church is actively involved with Campus Crusade for Christ where the "Four Spiritual Laws" are shared with college students on campus.

The Intellectual Style:

Some churches are offering Strategic Classes and seminars that ask questions people tend to ask or offer as to why they are not Christians, and then develop a logical presentation around them. Steve Brown of Key Life Ministries used to have "Bring a Pagan" nights where unchurched people were free to ask hard questions about Christianity, and he would try to answer them.

One church offers a "Discovery 1" course once a month on Friday evenings for newcomers to the church. Participants are invited to "Take their best shot". The team then responds to the questions offered.

Another church holds a weekly outreach event in a night club where attendees are invited to write down their questions about God on 3x5 cards. The events are appropriately called "3x5 Nights". One church offers a "Hot Topic Zone" within the church's courtyard where dialogue on hot topic issues routinely occurs. Another church offers a program they call "Quest" which is a Socratic, postmodern evangelism course for skeptics.

Other efforts include, book clubs, events for skeptics, basic Christianity classes, newsletters to unchurched families, attention getting book offerings sold in secular book stores, Internet chat rooms, and internet ministries to those interested in internet porn, and internet resources for people seeking to gain knowledge about apologetics. www.crossrds.org and www.xenos.org are two such sites.

The Testimonial Style:

One church offers a Saturday evening service called "The Seven" in which testimonials are a routine part of the event.

Another church uses video to present the testimonies during a service. "Straight Talk" is a ministry geared to businessmen in the community that features a lunch and a talk by a high-profile Christian.

"Strategic Saturdays" is a men's breakfast that is widely advertised and features testimonies of faith. One church uses testimonies at virtually every event. Some churches put testimonies into print and circulate them. Another church utilizes their web site to post testimonials of overcoming common roadblocks to faith.

The Interpersonal Style:

Some churches offer small groups in people's homes so unchurched people are more likely to attend. Others use "Matthew Parties" in the form of formal banquets, block parties, sports oriented gatherings, private dinners, and the like.

"Fast break" is one churches ministry to business men in the community who gather for lunch, interesting conversation, and drawings for restaurants, theaters, and sporting events.

Another church provides videos to its members to pass out to their non-churched friends. College age students are targeted by a "New Home" ministry of a church where the student is invited to spend time with a loving family from the church. Other opportunities include fitness classes, a couple's dessert night, "Punch or Tea" events that include Pay-Per-View boxing night for men, and a tea party for women.

The Invitational Style:

The Alpha course is an invitational approach example. Sunday services at noon to catch the late risers.

Another church holds "Summits" where unchurched men are invited by churched friends and relatives. A discussion of faith is included in the summit. Christmas pageants and "Love They Neighborhood" invitational efforts are also done by churches. Another church holds its meeting in a theatre. Budgeting seminars, Super Bowl Outreaches are further examples of what some churches are doing.

A review of the previous weeks' findings will be discussed with the participants attempting to draw some preliminary conclusions about potential evangelistic opportunities. *(Mittleberg: 247-323)*

Information Gathering Strategies

Successful operations depend upon good information. Gaining an understanding of the groups to be reached will be helpful in formulating the appropriate strategy. It may be necessary to acquire more information about some groups than others.

The key to success is knowing as much about what you are up against as possible. Moving into "enemy" territory to gather intelligence about the subculture and establish strategic alliances may be helpful. The preference would be to send someone to connect based upon an ability to speak their language. The objective is to gather as much information about the target as possible from within the group. Motorcycle enthusiasts for example, have a unique subculture of their own. They speak a type of language that is unique to them. They often have interests, wants and desires that are satisfied by their involvement with the motorcycle sub-culture. They even have a clothing preference.

Keep in mind, that Jesus would be in a lot of places where the average Christian would not go. Some are held by fear, some of that is self-righteousness, some is ignorance, and some of that is because we have been preaching a different gospel and lost touch with the heart of the message. Gaining information from first hand exposure is invaluable.

Magazines are a good source of behavioral information. Anyone wishing to fit in with those groups must look the part and speak the language.

A wide variety of other sporting interests also have unique characteristics, interests, likes and dislikes. Most general information about any sub-culture can be easily gathered. That goes for areas of interest ranging from basketball to witchcraft. The evangelistic efforts of a church can be advanced by understanding the unique attributes of the sub-culture. Far too often, people try to evangelize without understanding anything about the people they are trying to reach, or the group dynamics that are a part of the sub-culture.

Determine spending habits, lifestyle preferences, economic status, gathering points, common characteristics and traits of the sub-group, etc.

Certain web sites can be helpful as well in the information gathering phase.

The collaborative completion of the Session II: Potential Audience Grid. The grid is the place to determine if the potential option is Hot, warm, cold. A warmer prospect may translate into a strategy that moves quickly. A colder prospect may require significant amounts of time and energy before positive movement is achieved. It is also the place where one can determine if the party in each option, has a knowledge of Christianity, a degree of connectivity, a history, or a degree of resentment. Those factors, as near as they can be determined, will provide insight into the final selection of viable opportunities.

Complete the OPTIONS Grid of Potential Audiences (example)

EXAMPLE	OPTION 1	OPTION 2	OPTION 3	OPTION 4	OPTION 5	OPTION 6
Description	**PTA Moms**	**Lions Club**			**Bikers**	
Tactic	Join & build friends	Join & build			Join or Associate	
Evangelistic	Interpersonal	Interpersonal			Interpersonal/Intellectual/Confrontational	
Potential	Warm	Cold			Cold	
Roadblocks	ideology	Time			Behavior	
Impact Potential	Significant	Moderate			Significant	
Labor Intensity	Low	Low			High	
Availability of Intel.	High	High			Low	
Unique strengths	A mother	Leader			Strong masculine leader, ex-military	
Inherent weaknesses	none	Impatient			Tolerance of vile language	
Miscellaneous	Quarterly	Monthly commitment			Could be dangerous and will require the right temperament	
Style	(Groups within which relationships with specific individuals may be nurtured)				(A combination of inventory types)	

Remember the funnel concept. Your goal is for the number of options to be high. Do not place value on the merit prior to the 100-point test below. Prayerfully and completely fill out the grid and have participants score each option, considering all the factors, with 0 being the lowest and 100 being the highest. Add them up in order of collective ranking. Fill the new grid with the top-ranking choices.

FACTORS	OPTION 1	OPTION 2	OPTION 3	OPTION 4	OPTION 5
Description					
Tactics					
Potential					
Labor					
Intel.					
Unique strengths					
Weaknesses					
Misc.					
General Info.					
Rank 1-100 points					

FACTORS	OPTION 6	OPTION 7	OPTION 8	OPTION 9	OPTION 10
Description					
Tactics					
Potential					
Labor					
Intel.					
Unique strengths					
Weaknesses					
Misc.					
General Info.					
Rank 1-100 points					

FACTORS	OPTION 6	OPTION 7	OPTION 8	OPTION 9	OPTION 10
Description					
Tactics					
Potential					
Labor					
Intel.					
Unique strengths					
Weaknesses					
Misc.					
General Info.					
Rank 1-100 points					

FACTORS	OPTION 6	OPTION 7	OPTION 8	OPTION 9	OPTION 10
Description					
Tactics					
Potential					
Labor					
Intel.					
Unique strengths					
Weaknesses					
Misc.					
General Info.					
Rank 1-100 points					

S.T.E.P. 3
EVANGELISTIC STRATEGIES
Seminar III:

Scripture: Colossians. 4:5-6

Focus: Interactive discussion about specific groups or audience opportunities, roadblocks, anticipated degree of success of specific opportunities.

Aim:
1. Learn how to mine for information.
2. Review the Modes of Communication as a source through which information may be provided or mined.
3. Learn how to form audience specific strategies.
4. Discuss how to BEST communicate the gospel in each of the top options, given the information at hand.

In this session, a discussion of approaches will take place. The approach is to be determined by the best information obtained about the specific audience, and evidence that would suggest what will and will not work. A discussion about potential roadblocks or problems will also be accomplished in this phase. It is important to be honest with one another in the process. There are always individuals who will look at the initiative with an eye towards doubt and skepticism. They can be the critical factor in addressing and overcoming the objections to a specific effort. Use that energy to fuel solutions to mitigate the skepticism and doubt.

Key considerations: theatre of operation, needed tools, manpower, audience specifics, timelines, goals and objectives for each opportunity. The framework will provide information on obtaining pertinent demographics connected to virtually any subculture for evangelism. We will also use examples from the corporate world on how they gather relevant information. Such insights are readily transferable to the local church provided they have solid leadership and the passion for the lost. It will also thoroughly lay out possible considerations for implementing a strategy in any given context.

The preceding grid was completed and will serve to provide a visible way to look at the objectives to be achieved.

Each approach will include a detailed Strategic Matrix of goals, objectives, action steps and timeline factors for the groups targeted. One group may take a longer period to reach and develop than another. The Matrix will help keep the team on task with the objectives clearly before them. Once each of the steps has been taken and all personnel are in position, then the effort may be launched.

Depending upon the approach, the evangelistic effort may take place in a matter of days or over a period of years. Many churches state that they are missional. Far too few cast the net and bring in the catch. It is one thing to learn how to share the Gospel, and another thing to do it and execute. It is all academic if it is not practiced. Establishing reasonable time lines and specific areas of accountability will help in the execution phase.

The seven Fishers of Men phases below help to order and visually clarify what is to be accomplished and how. It serves as a thought primer. There is a subsequent grip in the next section that will be completed Complete the FISHERS OF MEN grid for each option chosen.

FISHERS OF MEN (Primer)

BASIC STRATEGY

① WHY	② WHO	③ WHAT	④ WHEN	⑤ WHERE	⑥ CATCH	⑦ REPEAT
Scripture	A. Audience	Bait	Timing	Venue	Decision	Disciple
Reasoning	B. Personality	**Intro. Bridge**				
	Hot	**Approach A**				
		i. Most Aware (Very aware of Christianity but not a believer)				
		ii. Benefit Aware (Understand the value to society, but not a follower)				
	Warm	**Approach B**				
		i. Solution Aware (Realize that Christianity has a solution for the ills of society)				
	Cold	**Approach C**				
		i. Unaware (No connection or understanding of Christianity)				
		ii. Problem Aware (Knows there is a social ill, but unaware of Christianity as a solution to the problems)				

Under number 2, you will see letter B and "Personality". It is at this point, when considering the strategy, personality traits, spiritual gifting, and life narrative are formed. This may be a stretch for some but it is the critical link in the entire S.T.E.P. system. All of us are shaped by our stories. Those stories, especially the ones connected to our salvation, can be used as a bridge to help others with whom we come in contact. This part of the seminar cannot be dismissed, ignored, or undervalued. Please give intentional time to building your own story. Even if it does not make sense to you, please complete it.

PERSONALITY

Pre-Frame

① BACKSTORY	② IDENTITY	③ STORYLINES
Character flaws	Leader	Loss and Redemption
Personal Struggles	The Adventurer	Us vs Them
Successes	The Reporter	Before & After
Failures	The Evangelist	Amazing Discovery
Victories	The Mom	Secret
Epiphanies	The Dad	Testimonial
Transformation	The Hobbyist	Third Person Testimonial
Polarity (Stand for something)		
The Champion	The Overcomer	
	The Boss	
	The Soldier (Etc.)	

It is important for every believer to be familiar with their own faith story. In column 1, you will notice a list. Communicating with others is most effectively accomplished when we are highly aware of our own deficiencies or flaws. People can relate to us when they sense a sincerity about us and an awareness of our own failings. Our struggles, victories and epiphanies help others connect to us. Identifying the transformation in us through faith in Christ, puts Christ front and center.

Our identity, how we view ourselves, what roles we play during our journey, can draw people in with similar traits. There are many storylines in our lives. The one that best describes our experience can be powerful. It is important for every participant to spend some time honing the aspects of personality that form a comprehensive storyline. Connecting the right person, with the right storyline, in the right environment with the right audience, can open an evangelistic effort and move it to success.

Keep in mind, the power of a compelling story. Jesus communicated and persuaded using stories. An indwelling of the Holy Spirit, combined with the proper story at the proper time has transformative power.

Under item number three, you will see, we ask the question, "What". That is a key question in the entire process. If the "What" is missed, there is not much hope for success. It goes to the issue of what time of connecting point makes the most sense for the specific audience and what approach, or series of approaches will result in the greatest opportunity to bring Christ into the relationship or conversation. When a prospective audience is unaware of your faith, the faith itself, the major tenants, etc., the approach must be different than an approach for someone who already has a grasp of the faith.

The Story Line process below will help fine tune the communication of a story that fits individuals, which is then plugged into the proper OPTION, and becomes a part of the strategy.

POWER

We all struggle. We all sin. Those that wear the battle scars of life struggles often have compelling stories. When communicated with intention and sincerity, those stories guide us to the ultimate story of redemption through Christ. The POWERFUL turning point in a storyline, is getting the audience off-the-hook of blame. A simple, but perhaps, challenging phrase, like, 'It is not your fault", can open them up to addressing the real culprit, the enemy of our souls, the one who comes to seek and destroy-the devil. The story can triangulate on that great biblical truth, and the storyline, through the power of the Holy Spirit, can move people to identify with Christ as the ultimate remedy for the trap the enemy has set.

Using the grid below, take some time to move through your storyline. Use bullet points under each heading. This will help keep your story succinct and provide a memory prompt. Now is not the time to pretend you are an angel, or put your best face forward. Now is the time to communicate your past. Some Christians will say something like, 'My past belongs in my past and when I accepted Jesus, it no longer has a place in my life". God will use your story to help others who are somewhere on the same storyline. Your story, connected to Christ, can be the difference between heaven or hell for someone else.

STORYLINE

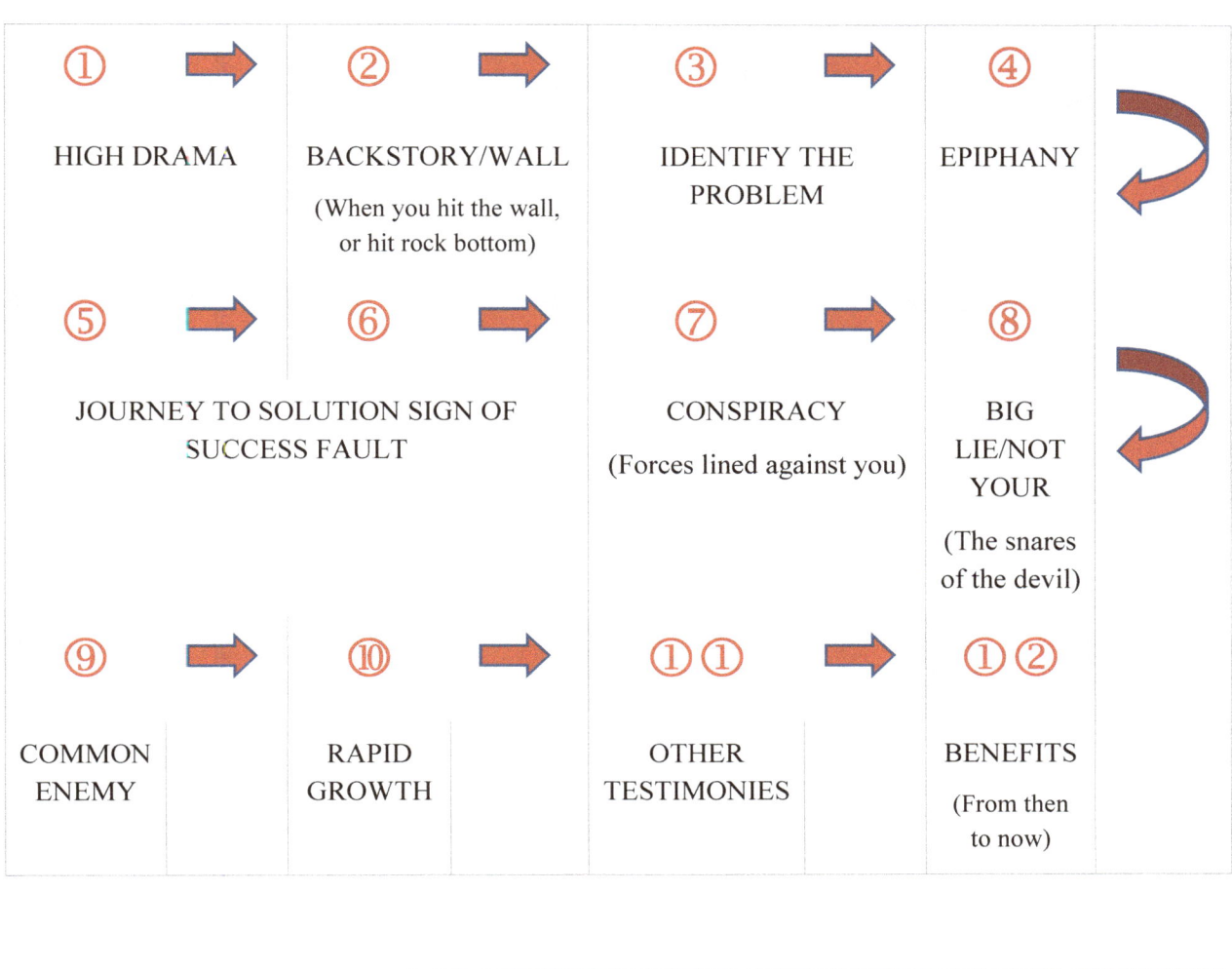

THINK-PAIR-SHARE

In small groups or within your group, think about your story, share it, and discuss your stories with an eye towards the possible areas of fit, in the options chosen.

The list below is to consider different modes of communication on mass initiatives. Some will apply and others will not. The list can also be incorporated into the strategies. It can also be used for social media strategies which can be very effective. More importantly, the modes of mass connectivity are primary sources of information. In our culture today, many of us live as open books to the world. We may not even realize the extent to which this is true. Anyone that spends time on the internet will see information on their screen, often related to searched items or products and services to which we opted in to, through an email. At no other time in our history, is more information readily available.

MODES OF MASS CONNECTIVITY

Mode		Vehicle	Viability
①	Direct Mail	U.S. Postal Service Email	
②	Networking	Internet	
		Mastermind Groups	
		Social Clubs & Organizations	
		Trade Associations	
		Support Industries	
		Facebook	
		Snapchat	
		Instagram	
		Twitter	
		New communication Innovations	
③	Television	Local Advertising spots	
		Channels	
		YouTube	
		Subscription base	
		Human Interest Story	
		Press Release	
④	Radio	Advertising	
		High market shows	
		Podcast	
⑤	Newspaper	Daily/Weekly Report	
		Press Releases	
		News Event	
		Advertisement	
		Blog	

S.T.E.P. 4
PLANNED STRATEGIES
Seminar IV

Scripture: Matthew 4:19

Focus: This is a step in which specific strategies for each option and audience within that option, is developed and mapped.

Aim:
1. Bring it all together into a workable strategy.
2. A force suitable for the unique characteristics of the specific audience. This is the point at which strategies become customized to the audience, with the completion of the grid from which the initiatives will function.
3. Participants will complete a review of communicating the gospel through the use of the bridge illustration.

DEFINING WHAT CONSTITUTES A STRATEGIC APPROACH

A strategic evangelistic approach:

1. Makes use of the best possible methods for the specific person or group. (Audience). It is also strategic when those approaches are based on solid intelligence, pertinent information relative to the audience.

2. Ensures an integrative approach, which means possessing a willingness to use any combination of strategies and tools at any given time for specific audience, to achieve optimal effectiveness.

3. Maintains a high degree of adaptability to the audience to be reached, with consideration for their interests, sensitivities, desires, and behavioral preferences, which therefore dictates the methods integrated into the strategy.

4. Builds awareness and sensitivity within the church, relative to the reality of diversity. It shapes evangelistic strategies to reach the unique groups.

5. Accumulate a working knowledge of an audience background, tastes, interest, priorities, intelligence and experience, which aids in bringing about evangelistic victories.

The seminar is to be participant driven, highly interactive, with the leader serving as guide for the discussion on what strategies to use for each option chosen.

From the previous sessions, collectively and prayerfully prioritize the audience options in order, with greatest consideration given to those options with the highest likelihood of success. The closer an audience is to awareness and general support of Christian tenants, the shorter the gap between non-belief and belief.

HOT	WARM
I	II
III	IV
MODERATE	COLD

KEY: Schedule your priorities. Determine priorities by the opportunities that will bring the best results in the shortest amount of time. Celebrate the small wins. Enculturate an atmosphere of celebration and praise for successes to come and for those that have already come to pass.

FACTORS	OPTION 1	OPTION 2	OPTION 3	OPTION 4	OPTION 5
Description					
Tactics					
Potential					
Labor					
Intel.					
Unique strengths					
Weaknesses					
Misc.					
General Info.					

A "point person" will typically manifest from the previous sessions, that would make the best choice as the primary face of the various strategies chosen. The balance of the grid below is completed by giving rough estimations. Hard timelines may not be realized and can therefore, demoralize those involved in the effort. On the back end of the grid, is

WHY	OPTIONS	WHO	WHAT	WHEN	WHERE	CATCH	REPEAT
Reasoning	PRIORITY I II III IV	Point Person:	Bait: Tactics	Timing: Start/End Duration 30-60-90 days +	Venue: Connecting Locations	Decision: Share story line, invite to a decision	Disciple Integration Strategy: Mentor Slow Fast Moderate
	OPTION A	A	A	A	A	A	
	OPTION B	B	B	B	B	B	
	OPTION C	C	C	C	C	C	
	OPTION D	D	D	D	D	D	
	OPTION E	E	E	E	E	E	
	OPTION F	F	F	F	F	F	

On the grid above, we start with "Why". What are the motivators that lead to choosing one specific option? Planning a strategy around an audience that is "HOT" in terms of their likely receptivity to the gospel, is significant motivation on its own. However, there are deeper drivers. Intrinsic motivators, based upon a deep seated internal desire, is easier to sustain than an extrinsic motivation. In working through the process, finding intrinsic motivation that is connected to the core of our identity, empowers the plan with greater resolve, resiliency, and commitment to see it through. Find a solid "Why".

"WHY" REFLECTION

S.T.E.P. 5
TACTICAL TEAMS, PRECISION PREPARATION
Seminar V

Scripture: Eph.: 6:10-18

Focus: Formation of team support for each initiative.

Aim: Review the strategies and build the supporting teams encourage the participants.

1. Form teams to support each point person.
2. Understand the qualities needed to function in the most supportive way.
3. Commit to ongoing prayer support of each initiative

No significant venture will be successful without the support of others. When a church begins to move towards mission success and fulfillment of the Great Commission, the devil will not be too far behind. Every point person will need constant prayer, accountability, guidance and wisdom.

Jim Collins, in his book *Good to Great,* provides a framework that is also applicable to the process. He includes four stages for development:

Stage One: Find disciplined people. Focus first on who is part of the team, then in what they will be engaged.

Stage Two: Find team members that are disciplined in their thought life.

Stage Three: Find team members with buy in significant enough to commit to difficult, tough, disciplined action.

Stage Four: Find team members with whom the system can continue to build.

Collins, James C. *Good to Great: Why Some Companies Make the Leap and Others Don't*. New York: Harper Business, 2001.

As support teams, the following guidelines are helpful to keep in mind:

1. Build and maintain a cohesive leadership team.
2. Create organizational clarity.
3. Over-communicate.
4. Reinforce organizational clarity through the participants.

Teams have life cycles characteristics. The leader and team members are tasked with paying attention to the life cycle of the team.

The Forming Phase is where questions of purpose, position, roles, and group dynamics are addressed.

The Norming Phase occurs when the team settles into a dynamic that collectively moves a mission forward.

Storming is the phase of maximum efficiency.

Re-forming in the process of evaluation performances and recommitting to the purpose.

Each team member is called to lead at a level beyond the norm. The leader must practice exemplary leadership. They should lead by modeling, leading by inspiring others with the vision of what can be. They should lead by challenging the status quo, lead others to act, and lead by instilling courage.2

To be exceptional, there are several qualities and virtues that team members and leaders can cultivate:

- Focus on results
- Promote meaningful change
- Guard your character
- Strengthen interpersonal skills
- Have organizational awareness
- Show respect
- Practice introspection
- Tune in
- Pay close attention to the systems

As a rule of thumb, it is important for those designated as part of the team, to focus on the above factors and take corrective action to ensure the project moves forward.

Leaders will also be quick to avoid the following dysfunctions that can disrupt progress:

1. Absence of trust
2. Fear of conflict
3. Lack of commitment
4. Avoidance of accountability
5. Inattention to results

Lencioni, Patrick. The Five Dysfunctions of a Team: A Leadership Fable. San Francisco: Jossey-Bass, 2002.

A team is only as good as its component parts. To have greater potential for team success, it is appropriate that each member of a prospective team be thoroughly analyzed. A combination of resources is available to help determine the strengths and weaknesses of individuals who are part of any given team.

The most important factors in success, were identified and written by the George Muller. Muller established orphan homes for thousands of children in England, and thousands came to faith in Jesus Christ. His work was a work of faith.

The work you are about to undertake is in every way, a work of faith.

1. Through prayer and meditation on the Word, be willing to let God have the glory if any good is accomplished by your service. If you desire honor for yourself, the Lord must put you aside as a vessel unfit for the Master's use. One of the greatest qualifications for usefulness in the service of the Lord is a heart that truly desires to honor Him.

2. Precede all your labors with earnest, diligent prayer. Do not rest on the number of tracks you have given because 1 million tracks may not be to the conversion of one single soul. Yet, a blessing beyond calculation may result from one single track. Expect everything to come from the blessing of the Lord and nothing at all from your own exertions.

3. At the same time, work! Walk through every open door, be ready in season and out of season as if everything depends on your labor. This is one of the greatest secrets regarding successful service for the Lord work as if everything depended on your diligence, and trust in the blessing of the Lord to bring success.

4. This blessing of the Lord, however, should not merely be sought in prayer, but it should also be expected. The result will be that we will surely have it.

5. Suppose that, for the trial of your faith, this blessing is withheld from a set from our site for a long time. Or suppose we die before we see much good resulting from our labors. Our labors, if carried on for in the right way, will be at last abundantly rewarded, and we will have a rich harvest in the day of Christ.

WHY	OPTIONS	WHO	TEAMS	WHAT	WHEN	WHERE	CATCH	REPEAT
			* Focus on results					
			* Promote meaningful change					
			* Guard your character					
			* Strengthen interpersonal skills					
			* Have organizational awareness					
			* Show respect					
			*Practice introspection					
			* Tune in Pay close attention to the systems EAM					
Reason	PRIORITY I II III IV	Point Person:		Bait: Tactics	Timing: Start/End Duration 30-60-90 days +	Venue: Connecting Locations	Decision: Share story line, invite to a decision	Disciple Integration Strategy: Mentor Slow Fast Moderate
	OPTION1		Team Members 1					
	OPTION2		Team Members 2					
	OPTION3		Team Members 3					
	OPTION4		Team Members 4					
	OPTION5		Team Members 5					
	OPTION6		Team Members 6					

Once each of the steps has been taken and all personnel are in position, than the effort may be launched. Depending upon the approach, the evangelistic effort may take place in a matter of days or over a period of years. Many churches state that they are missional. Far too few cast the net and bring in the catch. It is one thing to learn how to share the Gospel, and another thing to actually do it and execute. It is all academic if it is not practiced. Establishing reasonable time lines and specific areas of accountability will help in the execution phase.

Plans fail at times and succeed at others. We are still in a learning process. Each battle in the war for the souls of people, provides opportunity to gather additional information that could not be collected in any other way except in the arena. Experience is a great teacher. In the evaluation process, shifts in strategy may be developed to improve the outcome in future battles.

The teams are to expect and anticipate resistance. One of the key reasons so many believers are unwilling to share their faith, is the fear of rejection. We need to ensure that all personnel know and accept the fact that they will most likely suffer rejection.

Prepare emotionally and spiritually for resistance. We must labor to develop thick skins and soft hearts. We need also to understand that we are up against an enemy that will stop at nothing to keep the Gospel from having effect in the lives of people.

Those who follow Christ and become bearers of the gospel, will most likely collect battle scars. Jesus said, "Remember the words I spoke to you: 'No servant is greater than his master.' If they persecuted me, they will persecute you also. If they obeyed my teaching, they will obey yours also. They will treat you this way because of my name, for they do not know the One who sent me." (Jn. 15:20, NIV).

Prayerfully assign team members to support the point person.

S.T.E.P. 6
EXECUTING EFFECTIVE TACTICS
Seminar VI

Session VI: **Execution**

Scripture: Eph. 6:10-18

Focus: Execute the strategy and encourage the participants.

Aim:
1. Begin with Option 1 and initiate, or set the date for initiation.
2. Complete "to do" for each option chosen
3. Realign personnel or a shuffle the teams as needed.
4. Undergird each initiative with prayer for the Physical, Mental, Social, and Spiritual wellbeing.

Once each of the steps has been taken and all personnel are in position, then the effort may be launched. Depending upon the approach, the evangelistic effort may take place in a matter of days or over a period of years. Many churches state that they are missional. Far too few cast the net or haul in the catch. It is one thing to learn how to share the Gospel, and another thing to do it and execute. It is all academic if it is not practiced. Establishing reasonable time lines and specific areas of accountability will help in the execution phase.

Plans fail at times and succeed at others. We are still in a learning process. Each battle in the war for the souls of people, provides opportunity to gather additional information that could not be collected in any other way except in the arena. Experience is a great teacher. In the evaluation process, shifts in strategy may be developed to improve the outcome in future battles.

The teams are to expect and anticipate resistance. One of the key reasons so many believers are unwilling to share their faith, is the fear of rejection. We need to ensure that all personnel know and accept the fact that they will most likely suffer rejection. Prepare emotionally and spiritually for resistance. We must labor to develop thick skins and soft hearts. We need also to understand that we are up against an enemy that will stop at nothing to keep the Gospel from having effect in the lives of people.

Those who follow Christ and become bearers of the gospel, will most likely collect battle scars. Jesus said, "Remember the words I spoke to you: 'No servant is greater than his master.' If they persecuted me, they will persecute you also. If they obeyed my teaching, they will obey yours also. They will treat you this way because of my name, for they do not know the One who sent me." (Jn. 15:20, NIV).

S.T.E.P. 7
EVALUATION
Seminar VII

Scripture: Phil. 3:13-14

Focus: Review the strategies and determine what worked, did not work, and why.

Aim:
1. Evaluation or debriefing of each of the previous steps.
2. Overall evaluation of the strategies used and the results obtained to date.
3. Evaluation of participant changes.

Step seven can be taken in the middle of or at the end of an evangelistic effort. There may be times when due to factors unknown at the time of initiation, a review may be needed. Fine tuning the options, methods and strategies is an ongoing effort. Because the S.T.E.P.s is not a plug and play strategy, the intensity may be for more significant than an event, for instance. A high degree of adaptability is difficult for some people. Situations that may be fluid or unpredictable, will stretch people.

No system is perfect. There are always flaws to systems devised by man. When we neglect the prayer life that must undergird the process, our discernment suffers. Decision making can suffer, and effective execution may not manifest. As stated at the beginning of S.T.E.P. one, the Holy Spirit of God must lead.

Discussion:

1. What steps could then be taken, to ensure the right approach for each of the sub-cultures?

2. What would the rationale be for specific steps taken?

3. What shifts in strategy may be developed to improve the outcome in future battles.

4. What did you enjoy about the process?

5. What did you not enjoy?

6. How has your view of evangelism been changed?

7. Will you continue as an active participant in the evangelistic effort of the local church?

8. Evaluation or debriefing of each of the previous steps.

9. Overall evaluation of the strategies used and the results obtained to date.

10. Evaluation of participant changes.

CONCLUSION:

The process is more difficult in nature than those evangelistic approaches ordinarily used by the Church. No doubt there will be significant frustrations in the implementation of a strategy. Persevere through to the end. The requirement on the lives of the participants is significant. We would suggest an annual review of the specific strategies used, and a reevaluation of other options which may prove more successful. May the Holy Spirit guide you and may people come to faith in Jesus Christ, through your direct implementation of the S.T.E.P.s system.

Blessings!

Catalytic Leadership Academy

The Catalytic Leadership Academy is an organization committed to advancing the gospel message through the instrumentality of highly trained, skilled, and competent leaders.

To advance the reassertion of Christian values in a rapidly changing world requires strategic thinking—leading to global action at the epicenters of cultural influence, with excellence in execution within a multitude of disciplines. The Catalytic Leadership Academy is a catalyst toward that end.

Mission

The mission of the Catalytic Leadership Academy is to advance the knowledge, skills, competencies, and influence of present and potential Christian leaders across a broad spectrum of disciplines with insight and wisdom drawn from key leaders from around the world, to bring strategic advancement of the gospel of Jesus Christ.

Vision

The Catalytic Leadership Academy is an international force for the effective advancement of Kingdom influence by developing effective, passionate, and catalytic leaders across a cross section of disciplines in strategic locations around the world. It will develop and deploy creative strategies and methodologies across multiple cultural entry points worldwide.

Core Values

Christ First

- CLA values alignment with God's purposes above all other considerations.

- CLA values a Christ-centered focus and environment as an organization.

- CLA values an emphasis on grace and faith, over and above practices that tend toward divisive polemics.

- CLA values the unity of believers based not on differing points, but on points held in common.

Excellence

- CLA values a pursuit of standards of Conduct, Practice, Care, and Quality service that goes beyond excellent.

- CLA values a passionate commitment to expanding the positive influence of Christian values in culture.

- CLA values commitment to the dignity of all people, regardless of race, creed, or national origin, in so far as core biblical beliefs or matters of national security are not compromised.

Leadership

- CLA values an environment where leaders focus on continuous improvement organizationally and personally.

- CLA values the development of leaders who model and practice positive "can do" attitudes, encourage others to embrace risk, to dream, to believe, to dare and to do!

- CLA values the development of leaders who balance faith and reason with faith as the final factor in the tension between the two.

- CLA values the continuous development of leadership skills and practices that enrich interaction and accomplish the mission with integrity, good judgment, and innovative solutions with calm and clarity.

- CLA values leadership that reflects the character of the person and to those with whom there is direct responsibility.

Focus

Build

- To deliver customized education, mentoring, and strategies to reach specifically defined mission objectives.

- To become the preferred organization, recognized for excellence in educating and strategically mobilizing Christian leaders from the full complement of disciplines, with specific initiatives designed to penetrate cultures with the gospel.

- To prepare leaders with the skill sets, confidence, clarity, and resilience to lead themselves, others, staff, strategic functions, and organizations, regardless of pressures, challenges, or impediments.

- To collaborate with other educational institutions.

- To integrate insights from the Academy into courses through published books, articles, newsletters, magazines, and other social media outlets.

Unite

- To strategically unite Christian leaders toward the end that Christian values, attitudes, beliefs, and expectations gain significant integration into the social fabric and lead to cultural change.

- To bring key Christian leaders from a multitude of disciplines together for lectures, symposiums, workshops, and education related to impactful advancement of Christian influence in all levels of culture.

- To bring catalytic leaders from around the globe to challenge, inform, and inspire other Christian leaders to mission effectiveness.

Appendix A : Catalytic Leadership Academy

Deploy

- To forge alliances with likeminded, kingdom-focused organizations, through which our shared objectives may be achieved.

- To foster the development of enterprise opportunities that can make a strategic impact within specific target areas.

- To prepare leaders to be courageous, bold, ethical, resolute, resourceful, insightful, Christ-like leaders with a fierce passion for the advancement of the gospel through wisdom, love, mercy, and sacrifice.

- To operate in the Americas, Europe, Asia, and the Middle East.

Statement of Faith

- We believe the Bible to be the inspired, the only infallible, authoritative Word of God.

- We believe there is one God, eternally existent in three persons: Father, Son, and Holy Spirit.

- We believe in the deity of our Lord Jesus Christ, in His virgin birth, in His sinless life, in His miracles, in His vicarious and atoning death through His shed blood, in His bodily resurrection, in His ascension to the right hand of the Father, and in His personal return in power and glory.

- We believe that for the salvation of lost and sinful people, regeneration by the Holy Spirit is essential.

- We believe in the present ministry of the Holy Spirit by whose indwelling the Christian is enabled to live a godly life.

- We believe in the resurrection of both the saved and the lost; they who are saved will be resurrected to life, and those who are lost will face eternity apart from God.

- We believe in the spiritual unity of believers in our Lord Jesus Christ.

The Catalytic Leadership Academy

3583 Scotland Road

P.O. Box 391

Scotland, Pa 17254